COLOGNE

CHRISTMAS MARKETS 2024-2025

Explore the City's Xmas Bazaars And Have a Memorable Holiday Experience During the Festive Season

NATASHA D. VARNEY

TABLE OF CONTENTS

Map Of Cologne

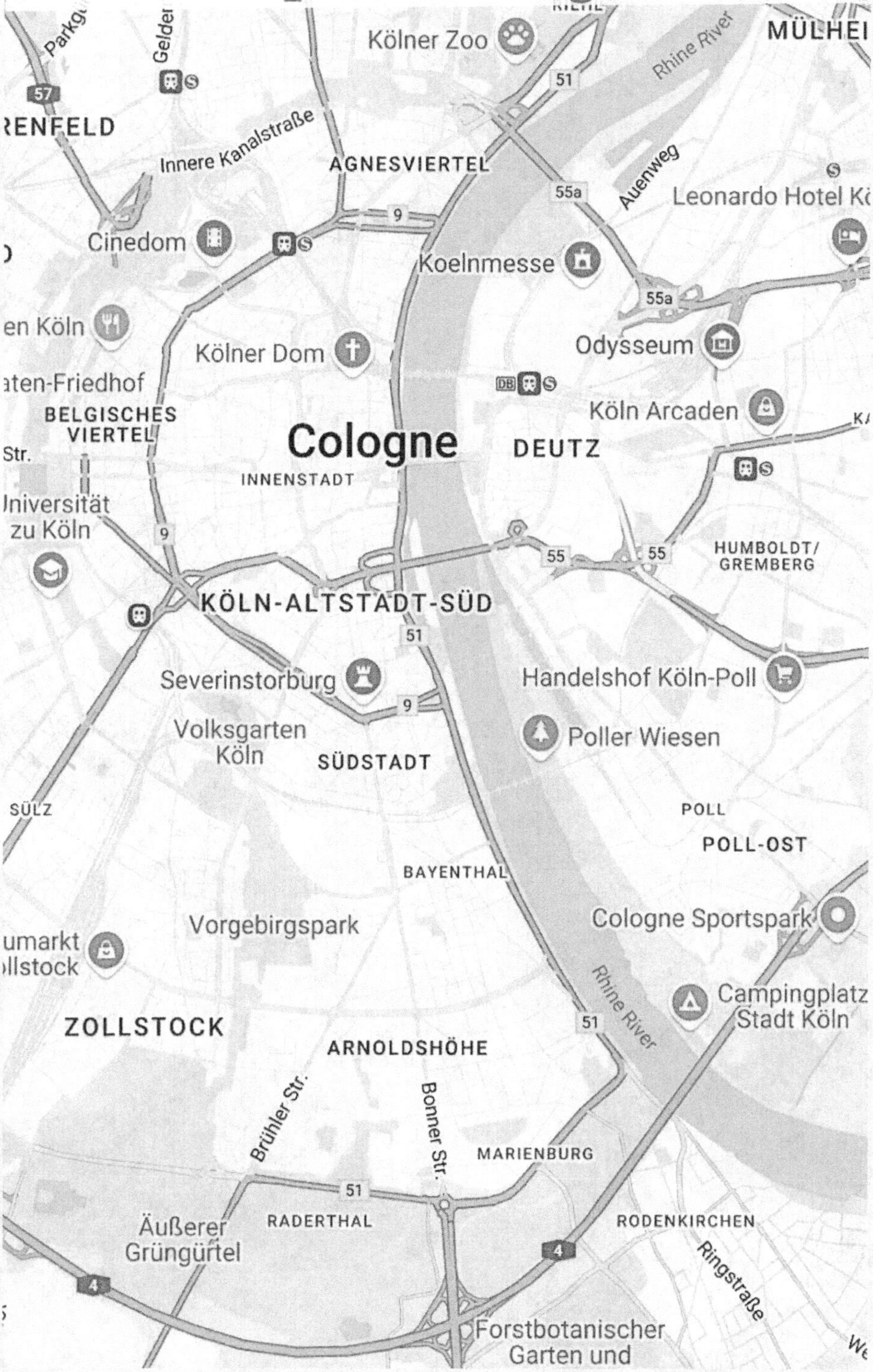

INTRODUCTION

As I stepped off the train at Cologne's Hauptbahnhof, the crisp winter air greeted me with a promise of magic. The towering spires of the Cologne Cathedral loomed majestically against the twilight sky, their silhouettes adorned with twinkling lights. It was my first time visiting the Cologne Christmas markets, and little did I know, this trip would become one of the most enchanting experiences of my life.

The festive spirit was palpable as I wandered through the cobblestone streets, each corner revealing a new wonder. The aroma of mulled wine and roasted chestnuts wafted through the air, mingling with the laughter of children and the soft hum of Christmas carols. It felt as though I had stepped into a winter fairytale, where every stall told a story and every light held a secret.

My journey began at the iconic Weihnachtsmarkt am Dom, nestled in the shadow of the grand cathedral. The market was a symphony of colors and sounds, with artisans showcasing their handcrafted treasures and food vendors offering delectable treats. I found myself drawn to a stall selling intricately carved wooden ornaments, each piece a testament to the craftsmanship and tradition that define this market.

As I sipped on a steaming mug of Glühwein, I couldn't help but feel a sense of warmth and belonging. The market was more than just a place to shop; it was a celebration of community and togetherness. Strangers exchanged smiles and stories, united by the shared joy of the season. It was in these moments that I realized the true magic of the Cologne Christmas markets – they have the power to bring people together, to create memories that last a lifetime.

One of the highlights of my visit was the Heinzelmännchen market in the Old Town, where the spirit of Cologne's legendary house gnomes came to life. The market was a whimsical wonderland, with fairy lights illuminating the charming wooden huts and the scent of freshly baked gingerbread filling the air. I spent hours exploring the stalls, each one offering a unique glimpse into the rich cultural heritage of the region.

As Christmas Eve approached, the city seemed to glow with an even brighter light. The anticipation was electric, and I found myself caught up in the excitement. On the night itself, I joined the locals at the cathedral for a midnight mass, the solemn beauty of the service a poignant reminder of the season's true meaning. Afterward, I wandered back to the market, now quieter but no less magical, and reflected on the incredible journey I had experienced.

Visiting the Cologne Christmas markets was more than just a holiday trip; it was an immersion into a world of wonder and joy. Whether you're a seasoned traveler or a first-time visitor, the markets offer something truly special. They invite you to slow down, savor the simple pleasures, and connect with the spirit of Christmas in a way that is both profound and unforgettable.

So, as you turn the pages of this book, I hope you feel the same sense of wonder and excitement that I did. May your journey through the Cologne Christmas markets be filled with joy, laughter, and memories that will warm your heart for years to come.

CHAPTER 1

BRIEF HISTORY OF COLOGNE CHRISTMAS MARKETS

Early Beginnings

The origins of Cologne's Christmas markets can be traced back to the early 19th century. The first recorded market, known as the Nikolaimarkt, opened in 1820 at the Alter Markt. This market quickly became a cherished annual event, enchanting locals and visitors alike with its festive atmosphere and array of holiday goods.

Challenges And Revival

Despite its popularity, the Christmas market tradition in Cologne faced significant challenges. In 1885, the city council decided to ban the markets at Alter Markt, citing concerns that the festivities had grown too large and noisy.

This decision marked a period of decline for the markets, as various attempts to revive them met with limited success.

It wasn't until the 20th century that the Christmas markets began to regain their former glory. In 1970, a Christmas market was reintroduced at Neumarkt, followed by the revival of the Alter Markt market seven years later. These efforts marked the beginning of a new era for Cologne's Christmas markets, setting the stage for their modern-day popularity.

Modern Expansion

The late 20th and early 21st centuries saw a significant expansion of Cologne's Christmas markets. In 1995, the iconic Christmas market by Cologne Cathedral was introduced, quickly becoming one of the most popular and picturesque markets in the city.

This market, set against the stunning backdrop of the cathedral, features over 150 beautifully decorated stalls and a large Christmas tree, creating a magical atmosphere that captivates visitors.

Following the success of the Cathedral market, several other themed markets were established throughout the city.

The Fairytale Christmas Market at Rudolfplatz was introduced in 1997, bringing a whimsical, storybook charm to the festive season. The Stadtgarten Christmas Market, known for its local artisan products and family-friendly activities, opened in 2006. The Harbour Christmas Market, with its unique nautical theme, debuted in 2011, adding a maritime twist to the holiday celebrations.

Cultural Significance

Today, Cologne's Christmas markets are more than just a festive attraction; they are a celebration of the city's rich cultural heritage and community spirit. Each market offers a unique experience, from the traditional crafts and culinary delights to the vibrant performances and activities.

The markets have become a symbol of togetherness, drawing people from all walks of life to share in the joy and magic of the holiday season.

WHY VISIT COLOGNE CHRISTMAS MARKETS??

❖ Festive Atmosphere

The festive atmosphere at Cologne's Christmas markets is truly unparalleled. The air is filled with the scent of mulled wine, roasted chestnuts, and gingerbread while twinkling lights and festive decorations create a magical setting. Live performances, including music and dance shows, add to the joyous ambiance, making every visit a celebration of the holiday spirit.

❖ Culinary Delights

One of the highlights of visiting the Cologne Christmas markets is the opportunity to indulge in traditional German delicacies. From savory treats like bratwurst and pretzels to sweet delights such as stollen and lebkuchen, there is something to satisfy every palate. Don't miss the chance to warm up with a cup of Glühwein, a spiced mulled wine that is a staple of the Christmas markets.

❖ Family-Friendly Activities

The markets offer a variety of activities that cater to visitors of all ages. From ice skating rinks and merry-go-rounds to craft workshops and storytelling sessions, there are plenty of family-friendly activities to enjoy.

These activities create lasting memories and make the markets a perfect destination for families.

❖ Handcrafted Gifts and Souvenirs

The markets are a treasure trove of handcrafted gifts and souvenirs. Artisans from across the region showcase their skills, offering a wide range of unique items, including ornaments, toys, jewelry, and textiles. These handcrafted goods make for perfect holiday gifts and keepsakes, allowing you to bring a piece of the festive magic home with you.

❖ Cultural and Historical Significance

Cologne's Christmas markets are steeped in history and tradition. The markets have evolved over centuries, becoming an integral part of the city's cultural heritage. Visiting these markets offers a glimpse into the rich history and customs of the region, providing a deeper appreciation for the festive celebrations.

❖ A Magical Christmas Eve

Visiting the Cologne Christmas markets during Christmas Eve is an experience like no other. The anticipation and excitement in the air are palpable, and the markets take on an even more enchanting glow.

Special events and performances are often held on this night, adding to the festive cheer and creating unforgettable memories.

❖ Accessibility and Convenience

Cologne is well-connected by public transportation, making it easy to reach the Christmas markets from various parts of the city and beyond. The markets are centrally located and within walking distance of major attractions, allowing visitors to explore the city's rich history and culture alongside the festive markets.

CHRISTMAS CUSTOMS AND TRADITIONS IN COLOGNE

Advent and Advent Wreaths

Advent begins on the fourth Sunday before Christmas and lasts for the weeks leading up to Christmas Day. During Advent, many homes in Cologne display an Advent wreath (Adventskranz), made of evergreen branches with four candles.

Each Sunday, one candle is lit until all four candles are burning on the last Sunday before Christmas.

In Cologne, Advent is a time for preparation and reflection. Families may gather around the Advent wreath each Sunday, light the candle, and sing Christmas carols or say prayers together.

Saint Nicholas Day (Nikolaustag)

In Cologne, as in the rest of Germany, Saint Nicholas Day is celebrated on December 6th. This is an important day for children. On the night before, kids leave their shoes or boots outside the door, hoping that Saint Nicholas (Sankt Nikolaus) will come by and fill them with treats, such as chocolates, nuts, and small gifts. If the children have been naughty, they may receive a rod instead, symbolizing punishment.

Saint Nicholas is often seen as the forerunner of Santa Claus and is depicted as a kindly old man in bishop's robes, carrying a staff. While this tradition is widely observed in Cologne, it is particularly celebrated in schools, kindergartens, and families.

Christmas Eve

Christmas Eve, known as Heiligabend, is a very important day in Cologne. It is when families gather for a festive dinner and to exchange gifts.

In Germany, the main Christmas celebration happens on Christmas Eve, not on Christmas Day.

A traditional Christmas meal in Cologne might include roast goose, red cabbage, and dumplings, or in some households, a simpler meal like sausages with potato salad. After the meal, families typically exchange gifts around the Christmas tree (Tannenbaum), which is often decorated with lights, ornaments, and tinsel.

Many people in Cologne also attend a Midnight Mass at one of the city's many churches, including the magnificent Cologne Cathedral. This religious service is an important part of the Christmas Eve celebration for many Christians, focusing on the birth of Jesus Christ.

Christmas Day and Second Christmas Day

Christmas Day (Weihnachtstag) and Second Christmas Day (Zweiter Weihnachtsfeiertag) are both public holidays in Cologne. Christmas Day, celebrated on December 25th, is usually reserved for quiet family time. It is common to have a special meal with close family members on this day. Traditional dishes vary but often include roasted meats, festive cakes, and plenty of sweet treats.

Second Christmas Day, or Boxing Day, on December 26th, is also a day off, and many people use this time to visit extended family or friends.

Some may also take the opportunity to explore the city's Christmas markets or enjoy the winter scenery along the Rhine River.

Nativity Scenes (Krippen)

Another beloved tradition in Cologne is the display of Nativity scenes (Krippen) throughout the city. These Nativity scenes depict the story of the birth of Jesus, with figures representing Mary, Joseph, baby Jesus, shepherds, and animals. Many churches in Cologne set up elaborate Nativity scenes, which attract visitors during the Christmas season.

In some cases, entire towns or areas of the city might have "Nativity walks" where people can walk from one Nativity display to the next, enjoying the creativity and detail of each scene. One famous Nativity scene can be found at the Cologne Cathedral.

Christmas Concerts and Events

Cologne is known for its rich cultural traditions, and during Christmas, many concerts and performances bring holiday cheer. From classical concerts in the Cologne Philharmonic Hall to festive Christmas choirs in churches, music plays an important role in the city's celebration.

Many of the city's theaters and concert halls also offer special performances of Christmas plays, ballets, and carol concerts.

These events are a great way for families to enjoy the holiday spirit together.

New Year's Eve (Silvester)

Though not strictly a Christmas tradition, New Year's Eve (Silvester) in Cologne is closely linked to the holiday season. The city celebrates with fireworks, parties, and gatherings. People often gather along the banks of the Rhine or on bridges to watch the impressive fireworks display that lights up the sky over the city.

Traditionally, Germans celebrate with a hearty meal, and many believe that eating certain foods, such as lentils or fish, brings good luck for the year ahead.

CHAPTER 2

BEST TIME TO VISIT?

Choosing the best time to visit Cologne Christmas Markets depends on your preferences and what you want to experience. Here are some key considerations to help you decide when to visit:

❖ Early Season (Late November to Early December)

Pros:

- FEWER CROWDS: Visiting in late November or early December means you'll encounter fewer crowds, making it easier to explore the markets at a leisurely pace.

- BETTER ACCOMMODATION OPTIONS: Hotels and accommodations are more readily available and often at lower prices compared to the peak season.

- FESTIVE ATMOSPHERE: The markets are fully decorated and operational, offering the same festive atmosphere and activities as later in the season.

Cons:

- WEATHER: The weather can be quite cold and unpredictable, so be prepared for chilly temperatures and possibly some rain.

❖ Mid-Season (Mid-December)

Pros:

- PEAK FESTIVE SPIRIT: By mid-December, the festive spirit is in full swing. The markets are bustling with activities, performances, and special events.

- EXTENDED HOURS: Many markets extend their hours during this period, allowing you to enjoy the festive atmosphere well into the evening.

Cons:

- CROWDS: This is the busiest time to visit, with both locals and tourists flocking to the markets. Expect bigger crowds, especially on the weekends.

- HIGHER PRICES: Accommodation and travel costs tend to be higher during this peak period, so it's advisable to book well in advance.

❖ Late Season (Just Before Christmas)

Pros:

- CHRISTMAS EVE MAGIC: Visiting just before Christmas allows you to experience the markets at their most magical. The anticipation and excitement in the air are palpable, and special events and performances are often held during this time.

- EXTENDED MARKET DATES: Some markets, like the Heinzels Wintermärchen at Heumarkt, remain open until early January, allowing you to enjoy the festive atmosphere even after Christmas.

Cons:

- VERY CROWDED: The days leading up to Christmas are the most crowded, with many people making last-minute visits to the markets.

- LIMITED ACCOMMODATION: Finding accommodation can be challenging and expensive, so it's crucial to book early.

❖Weekdays vs. Weekends

WEEKDAYS

Pros:

- Visiting on weekdays is generally less crowded, allowing you to explore the markets more comfortably. It's also easier to find seating at food stalls and enjoy the performances without jostling for space.

Cons:

- Some special events and performances may be scheduled for weekends, so you might miss out on these if you visit during the week.

WEEKENDS

Pros:

- Weekends are bustling with activities, performances, and a lively atmosphere. If you enjoy the hustle and bustle of a festive crowd, weekends are the best time to visit.

Cons:

- Expect larger crowds and longer wait times for food and attractions. Accommodation prices may also be higher on weekends.

❖ Evening vs. Daytime Visits

EVENING

Pros:

- The markets are especially magical in the evening when they are illuminated by thousands of twinkling lights. The festive atmosphere is enhanced by the glow of the lights and the warmth of the mulled wine.

Cons:

- Evenings can be more crowded, especially on weekends, and the temperatures can drop significantly.

DAYTIME

Pros:

- Daytime visits are less crowded, making it easier to browse the stalls and enjoy the activities. The markets are still beautifully decorated, and you can take your time exploring.

Cons:

- You might miss out on the enchanting evening lights and some of the special evening performances.

❖ Special Events and Activities

Many of the Cologne Christmas Markets host special events and activities throughout the season. These can include live music performances, ice skating, and themed nights. Checking the event schedules for each market can help you plan your visit to coincide with activities that interest you.

TIPS TO HELP YOU MAKE THE MOST OF YOUR VISIT?

1. Plan Your Itinerary:

Cologne has several Christmas markets, each with its unique charm. Plan to visit multiple markets, such as the Cologne Cathedral Christmas Market, Old Town Christmas Market, and Harbour Christmas Market. Check the event schedules for each market, as many host special events like live music, ice skating, and themed nights.

2. Book Accommodation Early:

Cologne is a popular destination during the holiday season, so it's best to book your accommodation early. Staying near the city center or close to a train station will make it easier to access the markets. Hotels and guesthouses can fill up quickly, so securing your lodging in advance will help ensure you have a comfortable stay.

3. Dress Warmly:

German winters can be quite chilly, especially in December. Temperatures in Cologne can drop to near freezing, and you'll be spending most of your time outdoors. Wear layers of warm clothing, a good winter coat, and don't forget gloves, a scarf, and a hat. Comfortable shoes are also a must, as you'll be walking around the markets for several hours.

4. Bring Cash:

While many stalls at the Christmas markets accept cards, some still only take cash. It's smart to have small bills and coins with you. You'll need cash for food, drinks, and small gifts. ATMs can be found around the city, but it's easier to have money on hand rather than searching for one while you're in the middle of the market.

5. Enjoy the Local Food and Drinks:

Indulge in traditional German treats like bratwurst, pretzels, roasted chestnuts, and gingerbread cookies. Don't miss out on mulled wine (Glühwein) to keep warm. Explore different food stalls to sample a variety of local delicacies.

6. Pace Yourself:

There's a lot to see and do at the Christmas markets, but it's important to pace yourself. Take breaks between markets to relax and enjoy the festive atmosphere. Most markets have cozy seating areas where you can sit down, enjoy a hot drink, and take in the surroundings. If you try to rush through everything, you might miss out on the joy of soaking in the experience.

7. Look Out for Local Crafts and Souvenirs:

The markets are filled with vendors selling beautiful, handmade crafts and Christmas decorations. From wooden toys to glass ornaments and candles, there are plenty of unique items to choose from. Support local artisans by purchasing their crafts, which make for meaningful gifts or keepsakes.

8. Use Public Transportation:

Cologne has an excellent public transportation system that includes trams, buses, and trains.

Parking can be challenging and expensive, especially during the Christmas season, so it's better to rely on public transportation. A day pass or short-term ticket can make traveling around the city easier and more affordable.

9. Exploring Beyond the Markets:

Take some time to explore Cologne's other attractions, such as the Cologne Cathedral, the Chocolate Museum, and the Rhine River. Consider day trips to nearby cities like Bonn or Düsseldorf for more holiday experiences.

10. Capture the Memories:

Bring a camera or use your smartphone to capture the beautiful decorations and festive atmosphere. Early mornings or evenings are great times for photos. Purchase unique, handcrafted gifts and ornaments as mementos of your visit.

11. Stay Safe:

Watch your belongings in busy places to prevent pickpocketing. Follow health rules, like wearing masks or keeping distance from others, especially indoors or in crowded areas.

HOW TO GET THERE??

✈ By Air

Cologne Bonn Airport (CGN) is located about 15 kilometers southeast of the city center and serves numerous international and domestic flights, making it a convenient entry point for travelers from around the world. To reach the city center from the airport, you can take the S-Bahn (S13 and S19) which connects the airport to Cologne Central Station (Hauptbahnhof) in about 15 minutes. Alternatively, several bus lines, including the Airport Express Bus (SB60), provide direct connections to the city center. Taxis are also readily available at the airport and can take you directly to your accommodation or the Christmas markets.

 By Train

Cologne has excellent train connections, making it easy to reach the city by rail from anywhere in Europe.

FROM WITHIN GERMANY: If you are traveling from another German city, you can take the Deutsche Bahn (DB) trains. High-speed ICE (InterCity Express) trains run frequently to Cologne from cities like Berlin, Hamburg, Munich, and Frankfurt.

These trains are fast, and comfortable, and often drop you off at Cologne Central Station, which is located close to the main Christmas markets.

FROM OTHER COUNTRIES: If you are traveling from nearby countries, the train is also a convenient option. Thalys and Eurostar run services from cities like Paris, Brussels, Amsterdam, and London to Cologne. The journey from Paris takes about 3 hours, from Brussels around 2 hours, and from Amsterdam about 2.5 hours.

🚗 By Car

Cologne is well-connected by several major highways, including the A1, A3, and A4, making it accessible by car from various parts of Germany and neighboring countries. While driving to Cologne is convenient, parking in the city center can be challenging, especially during the busy Christmas season. Consider using one of the Park & Ride facilities located on the outskirts of the city, which offers easy access to public transportation.

🚌 By Bus

Long-distance bus companies like FlixBus and Eurolines operate services to Cologne from various European cities. The main bus terminal is located near Cologne Central Station, providing easy access to the Christmas markets.

Cologne's public transportation network also includes an extensive bus system that can take you to various parts of the city, including the Christmas markets.

HOW TO GET AROUND THE CHRISTMAS MARKETS??

 ## Walking

Many of the Christmas markets in Cologne are located within walking distance of each other, especially those in the city center. Walking is one of the best ways to explore the markets, allowing you to soak in the festive atmosphere and discover hidden gems along the way. The main markets, such as the Cologne Cathedral Christmas Market, the Old Market (Alter Markt), and the Angel's Market (Neumarkt), are all easily accessible on foot.

 ## Public Transport

Cologne has an excellent public transportation system, including trams, buses, and the metro (U-Bahn and S-Bahn), which makes getting around the city convenient and efficient.

- TRAMS AND METRO: The U-Bahn and S-Bahn networks cover the entire city, with frequent services that can take you to various Christmas markets. Key stations near the markets include Dom/Hauptbahnhof (for the Cathedral Market), Heumarkt (for the Old Market), and Neumarkt (for the Angel's Market). Tickets can be purchased at stations, from vending machines, or via mobile apps. Consider getting a day pass if you plan to use public transportation frequently.

- BUSES: Cologne's bus network is extensive and can take you to areas not covered by the tram and metro systems. Buses are a good option for reaching markets that are a bit further from the city center, such as the Harbour Christmas Market.

Taxis and Ride-Sharing Services

Taxis are readily available throughout Cologne and can be a convenient option if you prefer a direct and comfortable ride. Ride-sharing services like Uber are also available in the city, offering another flexible transportation option. These services can be particularly useful if you're traveling with a group or have lots of shopping bags to carry.

Biking

Cologne is a bike-friendly city with numerous rental options available. You can rent a bike and explore the markets and other attractions at your own pace. The city has an extensive network of bike paths, making it easy and safe to navigate by bike. Biking is a great way to cover more ground quickly while enjoying the festive scenery.

Christmas Market Express Train

During the Christmas season, a special Christmas Market Express Train operates, providing a festive and convenient way to travel between the various markets. This hop-on-hop-off service allows you to explore multiple markets with ease, making it a great option for those who want to visit several markets in one day.

WHERE TO STAY NEAR COLOGNE CHRISTMAS MARKETS??

Hilton Cologne

Hilton Cologne is a modern and luxurious hotel just a two-minute walk from Cologne Central Station and a short stroll from the iconic Cologne Cathedral. This prime location makes it an ideal base for exploring the Christmas markets and other attractions in the city. The hotel offers a variety of rooms and suites, all equipped with modern amenities such as HDTVs, WiFi, and stylish bathrooms. Some rooms offer views of the cathedral. You can enjoy meals at the Pigeon Post Bar & Eatery, which serves breakfast, lunch, and dinner, offering a range of local and international dishes. There's also a grab 'n' go shop for snacks and drinks. For relaxation, the hotel provides a sauna and fitness area. Families traveling with children can benefit from the bespoke Family Experience, including a dedicated Kids Breakfast experience and a range of kids' amenities available upon request.

DETAILS:

Address: *Marzellenstrasse 13-17, 50668 Cologne*

No of Rooms: *297 Rooms*

Contact Line: *+49 221 130710*

Email: *info_cologne@hilton.com*

Hyatt Regency Cologne

Hyatt Regency Cologne is a luxury hotel situated on the banks of the Rhine River, offering stunning views of the Cologne Cathedral and the Old Town. This centrally located hotel is perfect for both leisure and business travelers, providing easy access to the Christmas markets and other key attractions. The hotel features 306 spacious rooms and suites, many of which offer breathtaking views of the Cologne Cathedral and the Rhine River. Each room is equipped with modern amenities, including in-room Chromecast, free Wi-Fi, and luxurious bedding. You can dine at the Glashaus Restaurant, which offers distinctive views of the Rhine River, Hohenzollern Bridge, and Cologne Cathedral, serving international and regional cuisine. Sushi lovers can enjoy freshly prepared sushi and sashimi, while the Legends Bar provides a cozy atmosphere for drinks and light snacks. The hotel boasts a modern fitness center, an indoor pool, and a spa, providing a relaxing retreat after a day of exploring the markets. With its proximity to the Koelnmesse trade fair and Cologne city center, the hotel is an ideal location for hosting meetings, conferences, and special events.

DETAILS:

Address: Kennedy-Ufer 2A, 50679, Cologne

No of Rooms: 306 Rooms

Contact Line: +492218281234

Email: cologne.regency@hyatt.com

Excelsior Hotel Ernst

Excelsior Hotel Ernst is a five-star luxury hotel right opposite the Cologne Cathedral, in the heart of Cologne's Old Town. Known for its elegant decor and exceptional service, this grand hotel has been welcoming guests for over 160 years. It features 134 luxurious rooms and suites, each designed to provide a comfortable and elegant stay, equipped with modern amenities and offering views of the cathedral or the city. The hotel boasts several dining options, including the Hanse Stube, which offers French gourmet cuisine with a Rhineland twist, and Taku, an award-winning East Asian-inspired restaurant. The Wintergarten serves patisserie and afternoon tea, while the Charles Bar offers a selection of wines, cocktails, and live music. The hotel also has eight stylishly equipped function rooms, making it an ideal venue for weddings, meetings, and special occasions.

DETAILS:

Address: Trankgasse 1-5 / Domplatz, 50667 Cologne

No of Rooms: 134 Rooms

Contact Line: +49 221 2701

Email: info@excelsior-hotel-ernst.de

CityClass Hotel Alter Markt

Cityclass Hotel Alter Markt is a charming hotel in the heart of Cologne's Old Town, just steps away from the Christmas markets. This hotel combines modern design with a touch of history, offering a comfortable and stylish stay. The hotel features elegant rooms with modern bathrooms, free Wi-Fi, satellite TV, a minibar, and a safe. Some rooms offer views of the Cologne Cathedral. A hearty breakfast buffet is served every morning in the spacious, bright breakfast room, which has a second level with a balcony. The hotel is just 300 meters from Cologne Cathedral and 500 meters from Cologne Central Station, making it an ideal base for exploring the city. The hotel's location in a historic area provides a unique blend of modern comfort and historical ambiance, allowing easy access to the Christmas markets, the Cathedral, and other key attractions in Cologne.

DETAILS:

Address: Alter Markt 55, 50667 Cologne

No of Rooms: 63 Rooms

Contact Line: +4902219201980

Email: hotel-alter-markt@cityclass.de

Hotel am Augustinerplatz

Augustinerplatz is a modern boutique hotel near the lively pedestrian areas of Hohe Strasse and Schildergasse, only a short walk from Cologne's Old Town and the Rhine. The hotel offers comfortable, modern rooms equipped with a TV with free Sky channels, a minibar, a safe, and free Wi-Fi. A hearty breakfast buffet is served every morning, and the hotel features a popular bar specializing in whiskey and vodka, which serves as a lounge for guests during the week. You can enjoy the adjoining wellness center for free, located 300 meters from the hotel. The hotel is within a 10-minute walk of Cologne Central Train Station, Cologne Cathedral, and the Ludwig Museum, making it a convenient choice for exploring the Christmas markets and other attractions.

DETAILS:

Address: Hohe Strasse 30, 50667 Cologne

No of Rooms: 53 Rooms

Contact Line: +49 221 2728020

Email: info@hotel-am-augustinerplatz.de

Hotel Lyskirchen

Hotel Lyskirchen is a contemporary hotel near the Rhine River and within walking distance of the Christmas markets.

This exclusive business and lifestyle hotel offers spacious rooms and flats in a prime location. The hotel features 105 modern rooms and apartments equipped with air conditioning, free Wi-Fi, a safe, minibar, and a hot beverage machine. The apartments include a kitchenette with a microwave and dishwasher. You can enjoy a delicious breakfast every day. The hotel offers an indoor pool, a sauna, and a fitness area, providing a relaxing retreat after a day of sightseeing. The hotel combines modern amenities with a central location, offering a comfortable and enjoyable stay.

DETAILS:

Address: *Filzengraben 26, 50676, Cologne*

No of Rooms: *105 Rooms*

Contact Line: *+49 221 20970*

Email: *lyskirchen@eventhotels.com*

Hotel Kunibert der Fiese - Superior

Kunibert der Fiese is a cozy 3-star hotel centrally located in Cologne's Old Town, close to Cologne Cathedral and the main railway station. Set on the historic site of a 13th-century tavern, this hotel has been providing traditional Cologne hospitality since 1879. The hotel features bright and spacious rooms with modern amenities, including cable TV and telephone. Free Wi-Fi is available throughout the hotel.

The hotel restaurant serves delicious Italian and international specialties, along with a fine selection of wines and the local Kölsch beer. You can also enjoy drinks at the Caribbean-style Aloha cocktail bar on the Rhine promenade. The hotel is an ideal base for sightseeing, shopping, or business trips, with several underground stations nearby providing easy access to all parts of the city. The hotel combines historic charm with modern comfort, offering a unique and memorable stay.

DETAILS:

Address: *Am Bollwerk 1-5, 50667 Cologne*

No of Rooms: *22 Rooms*

Contact Line: *+49 221 9254680*

Email: *info@kunibertderfiese.de*

Hotel Mondial am Dom Cologne - MGallery

Hotel Mondial am Dom Cologne - MGallery is a stylish four-star superior hotel situated in the heart of Cologne, just steps from the Cologne Cathedral and the Museum Ludwig. The hotel offers modern rooms with air conditioning, satellite TV, and free WiFi. Some rooms provide views of the Cologne Cathedral. The Mondial 1516 restaurant serves traditional and regional dishes, offering a culinary journey through German cuisine, while the Weinbar Legs 11 serves snacks and exclusive coffee specialties.

For relaxation, the hotel features spa facilities, including a fitness center.

DETAILS:

Address: _Kurt-Hackenberg-Platz 1, 50667 Cologne_

No of Rooms: _203 Rooms_

Contact Line: _+49 221 20630_

CHAPTER 3

EXPLORING COLOGNE CHRISTMAS MARKETS

Cologne Cathedral Christmas Market

The Cologne Cathedral Christmas Market (Weihnachtsmarkt am Dom) is one of Germany's most iconic and popular Christmas markets, located in the heart of Cologne, right in front of the magnificent Cologne Cathedral (Kölner Dom). This market offers a magical festive experience that attracts millions of visitors each year.

Set against the stunning backdrop of the Cologne Cathedral, a UNESCO World Heritage site, the market's towering spires illuminated with festive lights create a breathtaking scene that enhances the Christmas spirit. The market itself is beautifully decorated with thousands of twinkling lights, creating a warm and inviting atmosphere.

The Cologne Cathedral Christmas Market features over 130 stalls, offering a wide variety of goods. You can find unique, handcrafted gifts such as ornaments, wooden toys, jewelry, and ceramics. Traditional German Christmas treats like Lebkuchen (gingerbread), Stollen (fruit bread), and Bratwurst are available, along with the staple Glühwein (mulled wine). Local artisans showcase their crafts, providing an opportunity to purchase one-of-a-kind gifts.

The market is not just about shopping; it also offers a range of entertainment options. A stage is set up where choirs, bands, and solo artists perform Christmas carols and other festive music. There are various activities for children, including a carousel and craft workshops. An ice rink is often set up nearby, adding to the festive fun. In recent years, the market has focused on sustainability, using eco-friendly materials for decorations and promoting the use of reusable cups for beverages.

INFORMATION:

Location: *Roncalliplatz (in front of Cologne Cathedral)*

Address: *Roncalliplatz 1, 50667 Cologne*

Date: *18th, November – 23rd, December 2024. (Closed on Remembrance Sunday, 24th November)*

Opening / Closing Time: *Sunday to Wednesday (11 am to 9 pm), Thursday & Friday (11 am to 10 pm), Saturday (10 am to 10 pm)*

Heinzels Wintermärchen (Heumarkt and Alter Markt)

Heinzels Wintermärchen, also known as Heinzels Winter Fairytale, is one of the most enchanting Christmas markets in Cologne, Germany. Located in the heart of the city's Old Town, it spans two main areas: Heumarkt and Alter Markt. This market celebrates the legendary Heinzelmännchen, or house elves, known in Cologne's folklore for helping with household chores.

At Heumarkt, one of the highlights is the large ice rink. You can enjoy ice skating in a festive atmosphere, surrounded by beautifully decorated stalls and twinkling lights. For those looking for a bit of friendly competition, there is also the opportunity to try ice stock sport, a winter game similar to curling. If you're hungry, Heumarkt is the place to be, offering a variety of seasonal treats, from traditional German sausages and pretzels to sweet pastries and mulled wine.

Heinzels Wintermärchen at Alter Markt is more focused on handmade goods and decorations. Here, you can find a wide range of artisan stalls offering Christmas decorations, jewelry, and unique gifts. The craftsmanship on display is impressive, making it a perfect place to find special holiday presents. While there are a few food stalls, the main culinary delights are found at Heumarkt.

The market is divided into different themed areas, each with its unique decorations and atmosphere. Antique Alley, which connects Heumarkt and Alter Markt, is particularly charming, offering a selection of antiques and vintage items. The entire market is adorned with festive lights and decorations, creating a truly magical ambiance.

Heinzels Wintermärchen offers a diverse program of entertainment and activities. From live music and performances to children's activities and workshops, there is always something happening to keep you entertained. The market is designed to be family-friendly, with plenty of attractions for both kids and adults.

INFORMATION:

Location: *Cologne's Old Town (Heumarkt & Alter Markt Squares)*

Address: *Alter Markt, 50667 Cologne & Heumarkt, 50667 Cologne*

Date: *ALTER MARKT (25th, November – 23rd, December 2024)*
HEUMARKT (25th, November - 5th, January 2025), Closed on 24th & 25th, December

Opening / Closing Time: *11 am to 10 pm (daily), from 26th, December (11 am to 9 pm)*

Angels' Christmas Market

Located at Neumarkt, the Angels' Christmas Market, known as Markt der Engel, is renowned for its ethereal atmosphere and festive charm. The market is beautifully decorated with countless glowing stars and fairy lights adorning the trees, creating a magical ambiance. The stalls are designed to resemble quaint, fairy-tale houses, and the wide alleys invite you to stroll and linger. One of the unique features of this market is the presence of illuminated mythical creatures on stilts and magical angels, adding to the enchanting experience.

You can enjoy a variety of activities at the Angels' Christmas Market. Numerous stalls are offering traditional German Christmas treats, such as vegan spaetzle and Glühwein (mulled wine). Also, the market features live performances, including Christmas carols and festive music, which enhance the holiday spirit. One of the special highlights of the market is the presence of award-winning cuisine by Maximilian Lorenz, who offers delicacies like oysters and truffles. The market is also family-friendly, with activities and attractions suitable for all ages, making it a perfect destination for a festive outing with loved ones.

INFORMATION:

Location: *Neumarkt Square*

Address: *Neumarkt, 50667 Cologne*

Date: *18th November – 23rd December 2024. (Closed on Remembrance Sunday, 24th November)*

Opening / Closing Time: *Sunday to Thursday (11 am to 9 pm), Friday & Saturday (11 am to 10 pm), 23rd December (market closes at 9 pm)*

🎄 The Harbour Christmas Market

The Harbour Christmas Market in Cologne, also known as the Hafen-Weihnachtsmarkt, is a unique and picturesque Christmas market located by the Rhine River, near the famous Chocolate Museum. This market stands out with its nautical theme and modern design, offering a distinctive festive experience.

Situated at the scenic Rheinauhafen, the Harbour Christmas Market is easily accessible and provides stunning views of the river and the city. The market's layout features snow-white pagoda tents that resemble ships' sails, enhancing the maritime theme. This setting, combined with the twinkling lights and festive decorations, creates a magical atmosphere that is both modern and charming.

One of the main attractions of the Harbour Christmas Market is the large Ferris wheel, which stands at an impressive 48 meters high. This Ferris wheel offers breathtaking views over Cologne, including the iconic Cologne Cathedral and the Rhine River, making it a must-visit for both locals and tourists.

The market features around 70 stalls, offering a variety of high-quality goods and handicrafts. You can find unique gifts, festive decorations, and artisanal products, making it an excellent place for holiday shopping. There's also a large, real three-masted wooden ship where you can enjoy hot mulled wine, adding to the nautical charm.

Food lovers will love the Harbour Christmas Market, as it offers a wide range of fish dishes, fine food, and drinks from the region and around the world.

The market offers a varied entertainment program, including live performances, shanties, and pirate-themed shows, which add to the festive and nautical atmosphere. The "Lighthouse Spelunke" is a popular spot within the market, where you can enjoy drinks and music in a cozy setting.

INFORMATION:

Location: *South of the city center (next to the Chocolate Museum).*

Address: *Am Schokoladenmuseum 1a, 50678 Cologne*

Date: *15th November – 23rd December 2024*

Opening / Closing Time: *Sunday to Thursday (11 am to 9 pm), Friday & Saturday (11 am to 10 pm). On Remembrance Day (14th November), open only from 1 pm, and on Remembrance Sunday (24th November), open from 6 pm.*

🌿 Stadtgarten (City garden) Christmas Market

If you're looking for a smaller Christmas market with a festive atmosphere, the Stadtgarten Christmas Market in Cologne is a perfect choice. Located in the city garden on the edge of the city center, this market is a bit far from the Old Town and other markets, making it a unique and tranquil spot. Christmas time at the Stadtgarten in Cologne's Belgian Quarter is truly magical. Under twinkling lights and festive decorations, you can wander through this romantic market. The setting, surrounded by trees and away from the city's hustle and bustle, adds to its charm.

The market features over 80 vendors, each offering unique and stylish products you won't find elsewhere. These vendors rotate weekly, so there's always something new to discover.

From Christmas presents to craftwork and jewelry, you're sure to find the perfect gift. Food stalls at Stadtgarten are brimming with delicious dishes, including traditional cinnamon rolls, crepes, and Alsatian tarte flambée. For a unique taste, try the homemade mulled wine, which is sure to warm you up.

Stadtgarten Christmas Market has a more local vibe compared to other markets in Cologne. It's mostly visited by locals due to its distance from the main attractions. This gives the market a distinct feel, different from the more touristy spots. Though small, Stadtgarten Christmas Market offers a diverse range of artisanal products with a local influence. Its exceptional food choices and unique atmosphere make it a must-visit during the holiday season.

INFORMATION:

Location: In the Stadtgarten

Address: Venloerstrasse 40, 50672 Cologne

Date: 25th November – 23rd December 2024

Opening / Closing Time: Monday to Friday (4 pm to 9:30 pm), Saturday & Sunday (12 pm to 9:30 pm)

Nicholas Village (Nikolausdorf) Christmas Market)

Nicholas Village Christmas Market, also known as Nikolausdorf, is a charming and family-friendly destination located at Rudolfplatz. The market features an enchanted village with cozy half-timbered houses that create a relaxed and magical atmosphere.

Set against the backdrop of the medieval Hahentorburg, one of Cologne's last remaining city gates, the market is beautifully decorated with sparkling lights, red and green ornaments, and charming Santa and reindeer displays. The illuminated Hahentorburg, surrounded by traditional wooden stalls, adds to the magical feel of the market.

This market is perfect for a family outing, offering plenty of activities to keep both children and adults entertained. Throughout the day, the stage becomes the center of attention with performances by street artists and live bands. One of the highlights for younger visitors is the daily appearance of Santa Claus. Every day between 4 PM and 4:30 PM, Santa takes the stage to answer questions, take pictures, and talk to the kids. As the sun sets, you can follow Santa as he strolls through the village's alleyways, spreading holiday cheer.

In addition to the festive atmosphere, you'll find typical German Christmas market treats, hot drinks, and a variety of kid-friendly workshops and music shows.

Nicholas Village Christmas Market is renowned as one of the best Christmas markets in Cologne for families, thanks to its tailored activities and welcoming environment. If you're traveling with kids, this market is a must-visit.

INFORMATION:

Location: Rudolfplatz square

Address: Rudolfplatz, 50674 Cologne

Date: 18th November – 23rd December 2024

Opening / Closing Time: Sunday to Thursday (11 am to 9 pm), Friday (11 am to 10 pm), Saturday (10 am to 10 pm)

CHAPTER 4

BEST EVENTS & THINGS TO DO IN COLOGNE DURING CHRISTMAS

Christmas Concerts And Events

 Advent Concerts in Cologne Cathedral

Cologne Cathedral, one of the most iconic landmarks in Germany, hosts special Advent concerts during the Christmas season. The stunning Gothic architecture of the cathedral, combined with the heavenly sound of choirs and orchestras, makes these concerts truly special. Some of the most well-known concerts include:

- *DOMKAPELLE (CATHEDRAL CHOIR): This choir performs sacred Christmas music in various concerts throughout December. These performances typically include a mix of classical pieces, hymns, and carols, creating a peaceful and reflective atmosphere.*

- *ORGAN CONCERTS: The Cologne Cathedral also holds Christmas organ concerts, where you can hear the grand organ play traditional and contemporary holiday music.*

🎄 Christmas Concerts in Churches

Apart from the Cologne Cathedral, many other churches in the city hold special Christmas concerts. These are often free or request a small donation, and they provide an intimate and spiritual experience. Some notable churches hosting Christmas concerts include:

- *ST. APOSTELN CHURCH: Located in the city center, St. Aposteln Church is known for its festive concerts, including performances by local choirs and classical music groups.*

- *ST. PANTALEON CHURCH: This Romanesque church hosts Advent concerts with classical Christmas music, including performances by talented soloists and orchestras.*

🎄 Philharmonic Christmas Concerts

Cologne is home to the Kölner Philharmonie, one of Germany's top concert halls. During the Christmas season, the Philharmonie offers a variety of festive concerts:

- *CHRISTMAS ORATORIO BY BACH: This is one of the most famous classical Christmas pieces and the Philharmonie frequently stages performances of this work during the holiday season. It's a must-see if you are a fan of classical music.*

- *FESTIVE BRASS AND SYMPHONY CONCERTS: The Philharmonie also features orchestras playing a selection of festive symphonies and brass ensembles performing traditional Christmas music.*

Cologne Opera's Christmas Performances

The Cologne Opera House also gets into the holiday spirit by putting on special Christmas-themed performances. Whether it's a festive opera or a ballet performance like "The Nutcracker", the Opera House adds a touch of cultural elegance to Christmas celebrations.

Cologne Theatre Christmas Events

Several theatres in Cologne put on Christmas plays and musicals during the festive season. Popular productions include A Christmas Carol, children's theatre performances, and other family-friendly shows. These events are a great way to get into the holiday spirit, especially for families.

Classical Concerts in the Cologne Chamber Orchestra

The Cologne Chamber Orchestra is known for its outstanding classical performances, and during the Christmas season, they perform special holiday concerts.

These include classical renditions of Christmas carols, works by composers like Bach and Handel, and other festive music.

⚫ Christmas Circus (Kölner Weihnachtscircus)

The Kölner Weihnachtscircus is a popular event that combines traditional circus acts with festive themes. Held at the Cologne Fairgrounds, the Christmas Circus features acrobats, clowns, and animal performances, all set against a backdrop of holiday music and decorations. It's a fun and entertaining experience for the whole family. The circus runs throughout December and is a great way to experience the holiday spirit in a different setting.

⚫ Special Exhibitions and Events at Cologne Museums

Many of Cologne's museums also host special Christmas-themed exhibitions and events during the holiday season. Some even have live music performances or workshops where visitors can create their own Christmas decorations.

The Museum Ludwig and the Roman-Germanic Museum often feature seasonal exhibitions that tie in with the Christmas spirit.

Festive Cruises on the Rhine River

Cologne's position along the Rhine River allows for special Christmas-themed river cruises. These cruises offer a unique way to experience the city, with live Christmas music performances, festive meals, and views of the city's twinkling Christmas lights from the water. Some cruises also feature choir performances or brass bands playing holiday tunes, creating a peaceful and festive atmosphere on the water

OTHER BEST THINGS TO DO IN COLOGNE DURING CHRISTMAS

Visit Cologne Cathedral (Kölner Dom)

The Cologne Cathedral is one of Germany's most famous landmarks and is recognized as a UNESCO World Heritage Site. During Christmas, the cathedral looks even more stunning with festive lights and decorations. You can admire the beautiful Gothic architecture, climb to the top for an incredible view of the city, or simply attend one of the special Christmas services held inside.

Address: *Domkloster 4, 50667 Cologne*

Explore Cologne's Historic Churches

Cologne is home to 12 Romanesque churches, each with its own unique history and architectural beauty. Notable churches include St. Maria im Kapitol, St. Gereon, and St. Aposteln. These churches often host Advent concerts and special services during the Christmas season, providing a serene and spiritual experience.

Visit the Chocolate Museum

If you love chocolate, a visit to the Cologne Chocolate Museum is a must. Located on the banks of the Rhine, this museum offers fascinating insights into the history of chocolate and how it's made. During Christmas, they often have special events or chocolate-themed Christmas treats, making it a fun and delicious experience for the whole family.

Address: *Am Schokoladenmuseum 1a, 50678 Cologne*

See the Christmas Lights

Cologne is known for its incredible Christmas lights that brighten up the entire city. From the large shopping streets like Schildergasse and Hohe Strasse to smaller squares, the city sparkles with festive light displays.

Taking a walk around the city at night to admire the lights is a simple yet enjoyable way to soak in the holiday spirit.

Take a Day Trip to Nearby Castles

If you want to experience a fairytale Christmas, you can take a short trip from Cologne to visit some nearby castles. Schloss Drachenburg, located near Bonn, is especially magical during the holiday season, with beautiful decorations and special events. Many of these castles host Christmas events or markets, adding a unique and historical twist to your festive experience.

Ice Skating at Heumarkt

Cologne sets up a large ice-skating rink in the Heumarkt square during Christmas time. Whether you're an experienced skater or a beginner, it's a fun activity for people of all ages. The rink is surrounded by festive stalls, so after skating, you can warm up with a hot drink or snack from one of the vendors.

Address: *Heumarkt, 50667 Cologne*

Visit the Botanical Gardens

Even though it's winter, the Botanical Gardens in Cologne are still a beautiful place to visit during Christmas. Sometimes, the gardens host special light displays, making for a peaceful and romantic evening walk. The glasshouse is a great place to warm up and see exotic plants from around the world.

🎄 Explore the Old Town (Altstadt)

Cologne's Old Town is a charming area to explore, with its narrow cobblestone streets, historic buildings, and cozy pubs. During the Christmas season, the Old Town is beautifully decorated with lights and festive displays. It's a great place to enjoy a stroll, do some shopping, and soak in the holiday atmosphere.

🎄 Take a Ride on the Cologne Ferris Wheel

During the Christmas season, Cologne sets up a large Ferris wheel, usually near the Rhine River or one of the Christmas markets. A ride on the Ferris wheel gives you an incredible view of the city, especially at night when the Christmas lights are glowing. It's a wonderful way to see the festive city from above.

🎄 Enjoy Live Music and Entertainment

Cologne's vibrant music scene comes alive during the Christmas season, with numerous venues offering live music and entertainment. From jazz clubs to traditional German pubs, there's something for everyone to enjoy. Don't miss the chance to experience "Loss mer singe," a local tradition where people gather in pubs to sing Christmas carols and festive songs together.

CHAPTER 5

MUST TRY DISHES AT THE COLOGNE CHRISTMAS MARKETS

Glühwein (Mulled Wine)

Glühwein is a quintessential Christmas market beverage. This hot, spiced red wine is great for staying warm in cold weather. It's typically made with red wine, cinnamon sticks, cloves, star anise, citrus zest, and sugar. Some stalls also offer variations made with white wine or even non-alcoholic versions known as "Kinderpunsch".

Reibekuchen (Potato Pancakes)

Reibekuchen, also known as Kartoffelpuffer, are crispy potato pancakes often served with applesauce or sour cream. These savory treats are a staple at German Christmas markets and are perfect for a quick, satisfying snack.

Bratwurst

No visit to a German Christmas market is complete without trying a Bratwurst. These grilled sausages come in various flavors and are typically served in a bun with mustard or ketchup. The smoky aroma and juicy texture make them a crowd favorite.

 Currywurst

Currywurst is a popular German fast food dish consisting of sliced sausage topped with a tangy curry ketchup sauce. It usually comes with fries on the side. This flavorful dish is a must-try for anyone looking to experience a modern twist on traditional German cuisine.

 Flammlachs (Grilled Salmon)

Flammlachs is a delicious dish where salmon is grilled on an open flame, often on a wooden plank. The result is a smoky, tender piece of fish that pairs perfectly with a slice of bread or a side salad. It's a unique and tasty option at the Christmas markets.

Käsespätzle

Käsespätzle is a comforting dish made from soft egg noodles mixed with melted cheese and topped with crispy fried onions. It's often compared to mac and cheese but with a distinct German twist. This hearty dish is perfect for warming up on a cold winter day.

Maronen (Roasted Chestnuts)

Roasted chestnuts, or Maronen, are a classic winter snack. The chestnuts are roasted until tender and slightly sweet, making them a warm and satisfying treat to enjoy as you stroll through the markets.

 # Waffles

Waffles at the Cologne Christmas markets are often shaped like the Cologne Cathedral, adding a fun twist to this classic treat. They are typically served with powdered sugar, whipped cream, or fruit toppings. These warm, fluffy waffles are a sweet way to enjoy the festive season.

 # Hot Chocolate

For those who prefer non-alcoholic beverages, hot chocolate is a comforting choice. Many stalls offer variations such as hot white chocolate or spiced hot chocolate, providing a cozy and delicious way to warm up.

 # Stollen

Stollen is a classic German Christmas bread made with dried fruits, nuts, and marzipan, then sprinkled with powdered sugar. It's a festive treat that embodies the flavors of the holiday season. Slices of Stollen are perfect for enjoying with a cup of coffee or tea.

 # Gebrannte Mandeln

Gebrannte Mandeln are caramelized almonds that are roasted to perfection. These sweet, crunchy treats are a favorite at Christmas markets and make for a great snack or gift. The aroma of roasting almonds is sure to draw you in.

CHAPTER 6

SHOPPING AT COLOGNE CHRISTMAS MARKETS

Best Things To Buy At The Cologne Christmas Markets?

 Handcrafted Christmas Ornaments

One of the most popular items at the Cologne Christmas markets is handcrafted Christmas ornaments. These beautifully made decorations come in a variety of styles, from traditional glass baubles to intricate wooden carvings. Many stalls offer personalized ornaments, making them perfect keepsakes or gifts.

 Lebkuchen (Gingerbread Cookies)

Lebkuchen, or German gingerbread cookies, are a festive favorite. These spiced cookies are usually decorated with icing and come in different shapes and sizes. They make for a delicious treat and a charming gift. Some stalls even offer personalized Lebkuchen hearts with custom messages.

Christmas Market Mugs

Each year, the Cologne Christmas markets feature unique, collectible mugs for their Glühwein (mulled wine). These mugs often depict festive scenes or landmarks from Cologne and make for great souvenirs. You can keep the mug as a memento or return it for a small deposit refund.

Traditional German Toys

Handcrafted wooden toys are a staple at the Christmas markets. From intricately carved nutcrackers to charming wooden figurines, these toys are beautifully made and evoke a sense of nostalgia. They are perfect for children and collectors alike.

Candles and Lanterns

For those who enjoy home decor, the Cologne Christmas Market offers a variety of candles and lanterns. You'll find handmade beeswax candles, often shaped like trees, stars, or angels, and beautifully decorated lanterns that create a warm, festive atmosphere. These items are perfect for adding a cozy glow to your home during the winter months.

Wool and Leather Goods

Winter accessories like wool scarves, leather gloves, and sheepskin slippers are commonly sold at the Cologne Christmas Market.

These high-quality items not only keep you warm but also make practical and stylish gifts. Many of these goods are handmade from natural materials, ensuring they are both durable and comfortable.

Paper Stars

Paper stars, or Herrnhuter Sterne, are a traditional German Christmas decoration. These beautiful, illuminated stars come in various sizes and colors and are often used to decorate windows and homes during the festive season. They add a magical touch to any holiday decor.

Painted Porcelain Christmas Village Houses

These charming miniature houses are a delightful addition to any Christmas village display. Each house is intricately painted and often features details like snow-covered roofs and festive decorations. Collecting these houses can become a cherished holiday tradition.

Handmade Jewelry

For a special gift, consider purchasing handmade jewelry from the markets. Many artisans sell unique pieces crafted from silver, gold, and other materials. From delicate necklaces to statement earrings, there's something to suit every taste.

Christmas Pyramids

Christmas pyramids are traditional German decorations that feature rotating tiers with nativity scenes or festive figures. These beautifully crafted items are powered by the heat of candles and make for a stunning centerpiece in any home.

CHAPTER 7

USEFUL GERMAN PHRASES FOR COLOGNE CHRISTMAS MARKETS

Greetings & Polite Expressions

- Guten Tag!   *Good day!*

- Guten Abend!   *Good evening!*

- Auf Wiedersehen!   *Goodbye*

- Entschuldigung!   *Excuse me/Sorry*

- Danke!   *Thank you*

- Bitte!   *Please*

- Frohe Weihnachten!   *Merry Christmas!*

- Alles Gute im neuen Jahr   *Happy New Year*

- Einen schönen Tag noch!   *Have a nice day!*

Shopping

- Ich möchte....   *I would like...*

- Wie viel kostet das?   *How much does this cost?*

- Kann ich mit Karte bezahlen?   *Can I pay with a card?*

- Ich nehme das, bitte.   *I'll take this, please.*

- Ist das handgemacht?   *Is this handmade?*

- Ich nehme es.   *I'll take it.*

- Kann ich das bitte ansehen?   *Can I please look at this?*

Foods and Drinks

- Was empfehlen Sie?   *What do you recommend?*

- Ich möchte gerne zahlen.   *I would like to pay*

- Kann ich das Menü sehen?   *Can I see the menu?*

- Ist das scharf?   *Is this spicy?*

- Ein Stück Kuchen, bitte.   *A piece of cake, please.*

- Kann ich das bitte probieren?   *Can I try this, please?*

- Das schmeckt lecker!   *This tastes delicious!*

- Eine Tasse Glühwein, bitte.   *A cup of mulled wine, please.*

- Gibt es vegetarische/vegane Optionen?   *Are there vegetarian/vegan options?)*

- Können Sie das bitte für mich einpacken?   *Can you please wrap this up for me?*

Directions and Assistance

- Was ist das?

  What is this?

- Ich suche...

  I'm looking for...

- Wo sind die Toiletten?

  Where are the restrooms?

- Wo ist der nächste Geldautomat?

  Where is the nearest ATM?

- Wie komme ich zum Goldenen Dachl?

  How do I get to the Golden Roof?

- Gibt es hier in der Nähe ein gutes Restaurant?

  Is there a good restaurant nearby?

- Können Sie mir den Weg zum... zeigen?

  Can you show me the way to...?

Emergency Phrases

- Hilfe!

  Help!

- Ich habe mich verlaufen

  I've lost my way

- Rufen Sie die Polizei!

  Call the police!

- Ich brauche einen Arzt.

  I need a doctor

- Wo ist das Krankenhaus?

  Where is the hospital?

CONCLUSION

Thank you for choosing this guidebook on the Cologne Christmas markets. I hope it has provided you with valuable insights and inspiration for your visit. From the enchanting Angels' Christmas Market to the family-friendly Nicholas' Village, and the unique Harbour and Stadtgarten markets, Cologne offers a magical holiday experience for everyone.

This guidebook aims to highlight the best of what these markets have to offer, including festive decorations, handcrafted gifts, delicious treats, and memorable activities. May you enjoy exploring the markets and creating wonderful holiday memories.

Wishing you a joyous and festive season in Cologne.

Happy Holidays!!! 🎄 ✨

BONUS SECTION:

Christmas Shopping Planner

THIS CHRISTMAS SHOPPING PLANNER

Belongs to:

....

....

My Christmas
SHOPPING PLANNER

DATE: —————————

THINGS TO BUY	BUDGET	ACTUAL PRICE

My Christmas
SHOPPING PLANNER

DATE: _____

THINGS TO BUY	BUDGET	ACTUAL PRICE

My Christmas SHOPPING PLANNER

DATE: _____

THINGS TO BUY	BUDGET	ACTUAL PRICE

My Christmas
SHOPPING PLANNER

DATE: _____

THINGS TO BUY	BUDGET	ACTUAL PRICE

My Christmas
SHOPPING PLANNER

DATE: _____

THINGS TO BUY	BUDGET	ACTUAL PRICE

My Christmas
SHOPPING PLANNER

DATE: _____

THINGS TO BUY	BUDGET	ACTUAL PRICE

NOTE:

NOTE:

Made in the USA
Middletown, DE
23 November 2024